READING ABOUT

KW-054-350

Farm Animals

by Deri Robins

Aladdin/Watts
London • Sydney

J636
1360347

Contents

© Aladdin Books Ltd 2000

Designed and produced by
Aladdin Books Ltd
28 Percy Street
London W1P 0LD

First published in
Great Britain in 2000 by
Franklin Watts
96 Leonard Street
London EC2A 4XD

ISBN 0 7496 3966 0

A catalogue record for this book is
available from the British Library.

Printed in UAE

All rights reserved

Editor
Jim Pipe

Literacy Consultant
Ann Hawken
Oxford Brookes University
Westminster Institute of Education

Design
Flick Book Design and Graphics

Picture Research
Brian Hunter Smart

Meet the animals on a farm. There are pigs, chickens and ducks around the farmyard. Visit cows, sheep and goats out in the fields.

Then find out how dogs and horses help the farmer.

Farmyard

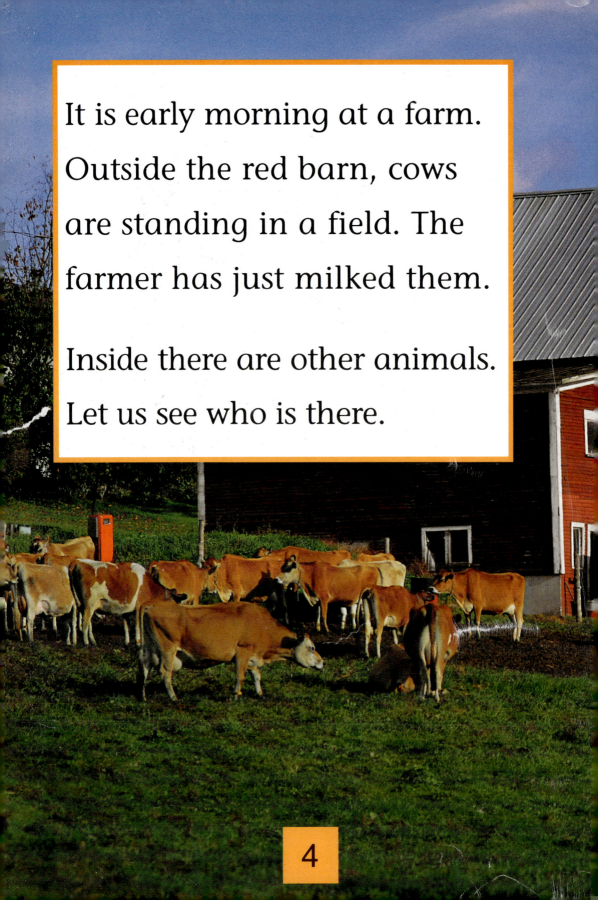

It is early morning at a farm. Outside the red barn, cows are standing in a field. The farmer has just milked them.

Inside there are other animals. Let us see who is there.

Farm

What animals are inside?

It is feeding time in the pig pen. The little piglets get all the food they need from their mum.

Piglets

Pigs eat all kinds of food. Some of them dig for food under the ground with their noses.

Pigs love to keep cool in a muddy pool!

Pig

In the hen house, hens scratch for seeds or worms in the ground.

Hens

Cockerel

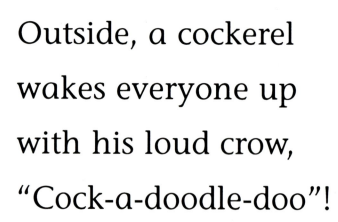

Outside, a cockerel wakes everyone up with his loud crow, "Cock-a-doodle-doo"!

Hens lay eggs, and sit on them for a few weeks. When it is time for the chicks to hatch, they break out of the eggs with their beaks.

Chick

Turkey

Where is its beak?

Turkeys live in a pen close to the farm. They are bigger than hens and ducks. Most turkeys have a flap of red skin under their beak.

Ducks waddle around the farmyard. Their webbed feet are made for swimming in the pond.

Ducks

Kids

The farmer often keeps baby animals in the farmyard.

Baby goats like to drink milk. It is like feeding a big, hungry baby!

12

Baby goats are called kids, baby sheep are called lambs, and baby cows are called calves.

Lambs drink their mother's milk. When they get older they eat grass.

Lamb

13

Cows

What are they eating?

These cows are milked very early in the morning, while you are still asleep in bed. They are milked again in the evening, too. Milking

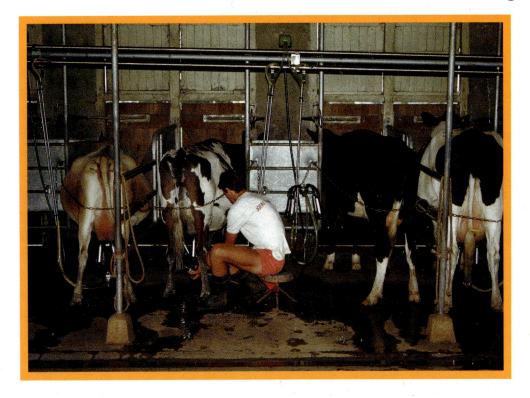

The farmer uses a machine to suck the milk from the cows.

15

Cattle

Would you like to live on a ranch? A ranch is a big farm where many cattle live.

A group of cattle is called a herd.

16

Do you know that cows are cattle mums and bulls are cattle dads?

Bull

17

If you are a sheep, your soft coat keeps you warm in winter.

This coat is called a fleece. The farmer cuts it off to make wool! But this does not hurt the sheep.

Sheep

Sheep and goats often live up in the hills, where the grass is too short for cows.
They live in groups called flocks.

Goats are nimble, quick and tough. They are good at climbing and jumping, too!

Goats

Some goats live on the steep
sides of mountains.

A farmer who looks after sheep is called a shepherd. This shepherd has a friend to help him – a dog!

Shepherd

22

Sheepdog

A dog is quick and nimble.

It helps the farmer move the

sheep from field to field.

The shepherd whistles to the

dog to tell it what to do.

Horses are strong, fast and graceful. Would you like to be a young horse running through the fields?

Horses

On big farms, farmers ride on horses to round up cattle and sheep. Some farmers keep horses just to ride for fun.

Pulling a plough

Not all farms are the same.

In some places farmers use horses, cattle or buffaloes to pull ploughs and heavy carts.

Buffalo

Llama

Some farmers keep strange animals. This llama from South America has a woolly coat like a sheep. It spits when it gets angry!

Can You Find?

Farm animals don't look like us. They have horns and beaks and tails. Can you find the farm animals that have these parts?

Beak

Hoof

Snout

Foot

Tail

The answers
are on page 32.

Clue: Look at
pages 7, 9, 12,
17 and 25.

Horns

Do You Know?

Do you know what things we get from each animal?

Llama

Sheep

Hen

Cow

Duck

Goats

Butter

Eggs

Wool
jumper

Cheese

Milk

The answers are on page 32.

Index

ANSWERS TO QUESTIONS

Page 28-29 – A chick has this **beak** • A goat has this **hoof** • A pig has this **snout** • A chick has this **foot** • A horse has this **tail** • A bull has these **horns**.

Pages 30-31 – We get **butter** from cows • We get **eggs** from hens and ducks • We get **wool** from sheep and llamas • We get **milk** and **cheese** from cows, sheep and goats.

Photocredits: Abbreviations: t-top, m-middle, b-bottom, r-right, l-left, centre. Cover, 2, 9, 10, 14, 28t, 28bl – Stockbyte. 1, 12, 17, 28m, 29b, 30mr, 30bl, 30br – John Foxx Images. 3, 11, 13, 31 all – Select Pictures. 4-5, 6, 8, 16, 18t, 18-19, 22, 26 both, 27, 30t, 30ml – Corbis Images. 15 – Christine Osborne/Corbis. 20-21, 23, 24-25, 29br, 30c – Digital Stock.
Illustrators: Wayne Ford – for Wildlife Art Ltd.